Start TO Finish
Second Series

Everyday Products

FROM Oil TO Gas

SHANNON ZEMLICKA

LERNER PUBLICATIONS COMPANY Minneapolis

Lerner Publications Company
A division of Lerner Publishing Group, Inc.
241 First Avenue North
Minneapolis, MN 55401 U.S.A.

Website address: www.lernerbooks.com

Photo Acknowledgments
The images in this book are used with the permission of: © Anton Starikov/Dreamstime.com, p. 1; © Huating/Dreamstime.com, p. 3; © Inga Spence/Visuals Unlimited, Inc., p. 5; © iStockphoto.com/Steve Froebe, p. 7; © Lowell Georgia/CORBIS, p. 9; © Wenbin Yu/Dreamstime.com, p. 11; © Dan Bannister/Getty Images, p. 13; © Lpm/Dreamstime.com, p. 15; © Visions of America/Joe Sohm/Digital Vision/Getty Images, p. 17; © Trip/Art Directors & TRIP, p. 19; © Lester Lefkowitz/Photographer's Choice/Getty Images, p. 21; © DreamPictures/Blend Images/Getty Images, p. 23.

Front cover: © iStockphoto.com/James Brey.

Main body text set in Arta Std Book 20/26.
Typeface provided by International Typeface Corp.

Library of Congress Cataloging-in-Publication Data

Zemlicka, Shannon, 1971–
     From oil to gas / by Shannon Zemlicka.
        p.   cm. — (Start to finish. Second series, Everyday products)
     Includes index.
     ISBN 978–0–7613–9185–2 (lib. bdg. : alk. paper)
     1. Gasoline—Juvenile literature. 2. Petroleum engineering—Juvenile literature. I. Title.
TP692.2Z46 2013
665.5'3827—dc23   2012008687

Manufactured in the United States of America
1 – MG – 12/31/12

TABLE OF Contents

Gas makes cars go. How is it made?

Workers look at the land.

Gas comes from a thick, black liquid called **oil**.
Oil is found deep underground or under the ocean.
It must be dug up. On land, workers choose where
to dig by looking for clues in the land.

Workers clear the land.

Workers bring bulldozers to land that may have oil. The bulldozers clear away trees and bushes.

Trucks bring tools for digging up oil.

Trucks bring tools to the cleared land. One tool is a machine that makes electricity. It powers a huge drill for digging. Another machine can pump up mud and rock from underground.

Workers put the tools together.

Workers put up a large frame. Then they add the machines to the frame. The frame holds the machines together to make a **rig**.

The drill digs for oil.

A worker runs the rig's drill. The drill digs a deep hole called a **well**. Some wells have no oil. The workers move the rig and try again until they find oil.

Pipes carry the oil.

The oil rushes up into the well. Machines pump the oil into pipes. The pipes carry the oil to huge tanks.

The oil goes to a factory.

Trucks, trains, ships, and long pipes carry the oil to a factory. The factory is called a **refinery**. A refinery looks like a maze of tanks, towers, and pipes.

Pipes heat the oil.

Hot pipes heat the oil. Then it enters a tower. The heat separates the oil into many parts. Gas is one of these parts.

The gas goes to gas stations.

The gas travels to gas stations in trains, trucks, or pipes. Workers store the gas in large tanks underground.

Fill it up!

At gas stations, drivers use pumps to fill their cars and trucks with gas. Then it's time to get back on the road.

Glossary

oil (OYL): a thick, black liquid found underground

refinery (ree-FY-nuh-ree): a factory where gas is taken out of oil

rig (RIHG): a frame and machines that are used to dig up oil

well (WEHL): a hole that is dug to find oil

Index

LERNER e SOURCE

Expand learning beyond the printed book. Download free, complementary educational resources for this book from our website, www.lerneresource.com.